Journey to Peace

A 12 Step Program for
Anxiety, Panic, & Life

Peace,
Peg C.

by
Peg Crompton

authorHOUSE®

AuthorHouse™
1663 Liberty Drive, Suite 200
Bloomington, IN 47403
www.authorhouse.com
Phone: 1-800-839-8640

First published by AuthorHouse 10/22/2008

ISBN: 978-1-4389-2365-9 (sc)

Printed in the United States of America
Bloomington, Indiana

This book is printed on acid-free paper.

Preface

Journey to Peace is a twelve-step program with tried and true methods for reducing symptoms of anxiety, panic, and everyday stress. Success in this program, like any other, is best achieved with the guidance and support of a health care professional.

This is not a prescription to follow exactly. It is not necessary for the reader to implement every piece of advice or even complete each step. Instead, readers are encouraged to take what works for them and apply in ways that reap the most benefits.

In addition to the twelve steps, this book offers cognitive behavioral techniques that will help to reduce stress and promote relaxation. These techniques can be found at the end of the book, immediately following the twelve steps.

Introduction

Many books have been written on the subjects of anxiety and panic. Members of the medical profession have written most of them. The information obtained from these books is educational, informative, and stems from years of study, research and medical practice methodology.

The Journey to Peace takes an entirely different approach. Written by a lay person with years of experience in dealing with anxiety, it is intended to show a clearer perspective.

Readers will not find an in-depth definition or explanation of these conditions. Instead, practical steps to deal with anxiety are presented in a clear, concise, easy to read format.

These twelve steps took shape through many years of practicing different techniques, reading about and studying the subject, and personal experiences of the author. Each of these steps plays a role in reducing the physical, mental, and emotional effects of stress, anxiety, and panic.

This book is written to reach out and help others that experience symptoms of anxiety and panic. It is my greatest expectation that this book has come to fruition in order to reach those that will benefit from it the most.

I sincerely hope that the practice of these twelve steps will provide some guidance and relief. Godspeed as you embark on this journey to peace. You may begin your journey now.

The 12 Steps

J--Journal

O--Outreach

U--Understand

R--Reconsider

N--Navigate

E--Exercise

Y—Yield

to

P--Practice

E--Encouragement

A--Attitude

C--Create

E--Extravagance

Chapter 1

Step 1

Journal

Journal writing is an age-old tradition that serves many purposes. Journals can document historical events, provide family genealogy information, assist in solving crimes, allow those writing to vent feelings, help in remembering past events, give us writing practice, and supply support for self-improvement.

Due to the advance of technology and today's busy lifestyles, writing in a journal using pen and paper has become a rare practice. We see it more on television and in movies than in everyday life.

Journal writing is often portrayed as a very personal, private practice. Family and friends seldom share or pass on journals. Reading others personal writing is considered rude and inappropriate.

When most of us think of journals, we think of the stereotypical diary. We tend to picture a bound book with a strap and key, or a hard-back notebook with a pretty cover that gets written in at the end of the day.

If we begin to think of journaling in a less conventional way and utilize it as a valuable tool, it can be one of the single, most important things that we do. Do not underestimate the power of keeping a journal.

In this first step of the journey it is recommended that you keep three separate journals, or use a three subject notebook. This is not as overwhelming as it sounds. It is not necessary to practice journal writing like a religion. You need not write in it every day. It is, quite simply, a tool to use when most needed.

Why three, you ask? Okay, I'll explain. Part one of your journal, or journal number one, should be used to document all physical, mental, and emotional symptoms that you experience. When you find yourself symptomatic, pay particular attention to what you are feeling and jot it all down. Be sure to include the date, day of the week, time of day, triggers, stressors, and any foods you've eaten beforehand. This helps you to establish patterns, track what is happening to you, and provides important information to share with health care providers.

If you go to a doctor's office with a journal of your symptoms and are able to clearly articulate all of your concerns, you just may contribute to a more accurate diagnosis. When you do not keep a journal it is difficult to determine patterns and relay information to the doctor. It is too easy to forget or omit symptoms, especially if you are not symptomatic by the time you get to the doctor's office.

Part one of this journal is so important that I cannot stipulate it enough. It's a beneficial tool for any illness, but especially for symptoms of anxiety and/or panic. I'll explain more about that in the next chapter.

For the second part of the journal, or journal number two, you should keep track of any recurring dreams or nightmares that you have. Many people who suffer from anxiety and panic have trouble sleeping and have frequent nightmares, scary, or recurring dreams. Most dreams simply stem from unresolved issues of the day.

The anxious mind is always thinking and these thoughts can become a circus in your head when you sleep. This only becomes a major problem if it constantly awakens you and you cannot get enough rest.

For the most part dreams are forgotten quickly; however, there are dreams that can haunt you or increase anxious feelings. The practice of writing them down can help to establish dreaming patterns and bring to light any unresolved issues. For example, if you are dreaming about urinating in your bed all night long, perhaps you can decide to stop taking in any fluids two hours before bed and see if that helps.

Keep in mind that focusing on dreams too much and attempting to interpret them can cause more anxiety. The practice of writing them down is to help ease anxiety. It's meant to assist you in letting go of the dreams and/or resolve any issues that may be contributing to the anxiety that is coming out in your dreams.

Try to remember that some dreams are just dreams. They all don't have to have some hidden meaning that you need to respond to. If your dreams are enjoyable and not causing you any stress, then you don't need this second journal.

The third part of the journal, or journal number three is a grateful journal. A grateful journal is one where you write down at least one thing that you are grateful for. It can be anything. Maybe you're grateful for a hot cup of tea, a hot shower, a friendship, or having a good book to read.

This particular journal almost serves as a form of meditation. It is especially helpful to work with this when you are feeling stressed. It can also be a good way to begin or end a day, or week, or month. There are no rules as to how often you should write in this one, but you may find it so beneficial that you want to add something on a daily basis.

A grateful journal allows the mind to shift to something positive. It can take you away from worry and stress and remind you to stop to notice and enjoy the little things in life. Again, don't underestimate the power of a journal like this. It can change your perspective on life and open channels you never knew were there.

This happens to be my favorite type of journal writing. I will sometimes find myself grateful for twenty-five things in one day. A few examples are: swirling leaves on the pavement, a family of deer drinking from a stream, a line of school busses full of excited children at the end of a school day, dogs playing together, the quiet hum of the furnace, a clear sky with bright stars and a quarter moon, the feel of clean sheets, freshly fallen snow, the sound of rain on the roof, bird songs, blooming flowers, and more. The list can be never-ending. It can include anything from important milestones to the smallest moment.

If you find it easier, begin with one journal and add as you go along and get used to writing. It won't be long before you reach for one automatically as you'll begin to see how helpful it is. I strongly suggest that if you choose to keep just one journal you make it your symptom diary.

Once you practice awhile, you may just find yourself coming up with other creative ideas for journal writing. There are hobby journals, scrap-booking, career journals, and family journals. Journal writing is an important tool for stress, anxiety, and/or panic, and also an important tool for life.

Chapter 2

Step 2

Outreach

When you have completed your symptom journal, or have kept it for approximately one month, you should have enough information to begin an outreach effort. It is better to track symptoms over time to see if any patterns emerge, but you do not want to wait too long before you reach out for assistance. This one month mark is an estimate. In some cases, it may take a week and in others may take two months. It all depends on the frequency of your symptoms.

Tracking symptoms in this manner may bring you to a few realizations on your own. It's quite possible that you recognize patterns or triggers just by writing them down and looking at them. It can create an ah-ha moment, especially if you respond to your anxiety symptoms by fighting them or denying their existence. Seeing your experiences in black and white, written on plain paper can change your perspective rather quickly. It's a simple act that can make an amazing difference.

Begin your outreach effort by getting a recommendation for a good diagnostic doctor. Ask family, friends, and associates who they have had success with. You'll want to start with a family doctor, general practitioner, or an internal medicine specialist. Check with your insurance company to make sure they will cover the visit. Make an appointment, arrive on time, and bring your journal with you. Also bring any questions you may have for the doctor.

Any good physician will do the following: listen intently, pay attention to your concerns, answer any questions you have, read your journal of symptoms, and suggest some testing. At the very least, the doctor should do these five basics: get your weight, temperature, vital signs, and order a complete blood count and urinalysis.

Trust your instincts when it comes to the doctor. If you do not agree with what you hear or feel this may not be the right doctor for you, then get a second opinion. I prefer a physician that treats me as an equal and a human being. It bothers me when a doctor seems to be simply playing the role of doctor and treats me as a patient or diagnosis. It is better to have a physician that will work with you to determine what may be wrong, if anything, and to discuss treatment options. It can make a big difference to you if you have a doctor that seems genuinely concerned and truly wants to help, without making any judgment of personal character or jumping to any conclusions without a thorough physical work-up.

If the doctor declares that you are healthy, and finds nothing wrong with you physically, then he/she may refer you to a psychiatrist. If the doctor suspects an anxiety disorder, then it is better to get a referral. Although some general doctors can and will prescribe medicines for anxiety related disorders, it is better to see a specialist. The specialist, or psychiatrist, will have specific, in-depth training in this area, and will know more about the most current medications and treatment options available.

Again, check with your insurance company for coverage and make an appointment with the psychiatrist. Remember to bring your journal, and any records you may have from the previous doctor visit.

At your first psychiatric appointment spend a few minutes getting to know the doctor. Ask any questions you may have. If you are uncomfortable with the doctor's responses and/or find that you don't think this doctor is the right one for you, find another one. It is okay to interview doctors until you find the right one.

Be forewarned; however, most psychiatrists will discourage you from shopping around. They don't like you to switch doctors. There are good, solid reasons for this. Among them are: treatment can become inconsistent, patients can become confused by differences in opinion on what the best treatment is, and patients may suffer more by following more than one recommendation at a time. In the beginning, however, I see no harm in seeking a second opinion or searching until you find a doctor that you are comfortable with. After all, if you have anxiety about your physician, then how does that help you?

Keep in mind that psychiatrists don't typically engage in talk therapy. They evaluate your symptoms, read your body language, listen, and usually prescribe medications that may help you. Be sure to ask about the effectiveness of certain treatments, side effects, and duration of treatment. Don't hesitate to ask a psychiatrist what his or her specialty is. If you have been diagnosed with an anxiety disorder, you may choose to see a psychiatrist that specializes in anxiety disorders.

If you prefer not to take medications, are sensitive to side effects, or wish to pursue another method of treatment, ask for a referral. There are psychologists that specialize in cognitive behavior techniques. Sometimes these techniques work well and medication is not necessary. In other instances, a combination of medicines and cognitive behavior techniques is more effective.

When anxiety or panic is caused by life stressors that may be temporary in nature, talk therapy may be enough to see you through. In difficult times it sometimes helps to have someone objective to talk with. Reassurance and comfort is often easier to accept from someone that is not emotionally involved. This is especially true if the stress stems from events that are perceived as socially unacceptable. Perhaps the issue you are facing is something a counselor specializes in. Examples of this are: loved ones dealing with alcohol or drug abuse, domestic violence, sexual assault or extended grief over the loss of someone special. Psychologists, licensed clinical social workers, and counselors are professionally trained to deal with these types of issues. They also have specialties, so be sure to find one that has extensive training and/ or experience with the specific concern that you have.

Follow whatever course of treatment works best for you. Try to be patient with the process. It may take time to get a definitive diagnosis and find the correct treatment plan. Know that it will take time and effort to see improvement. Have confidence that you are moving in the right direction. You may find, before too long, that anxiety no longer has a hold on you and that you are in control of your reactions to anxiety.

Chapter 3

Step 3

Understand

Understanding and acceptance are key components in dealing with anxiety and panic. If you do not understand what is happening to you or if you are not willing to accept it once you do, then the anxiety will feed on itself and escalate.

If you have completed the first two steps at this point, you should have a pretty good idea about what you are dealing with. Writing in a journal should give you clear insight to your physical, mental, and emotional symptoms. Seeking assistance from the medical profession has given you the opportunity to get a definitive diagnosis and rule out physical causes for your symptoms.

When more than one doctor agrees that you are dealing with an anxiety disorder then it is time to understand and accept. Acceptance usually comes after understanding. Understanding comes from knowledge. Knowledge comes from information, and information is power.

So, where do you begin with this step? I'm glad you asked. Begin by gathering information. Find a couple of good web sites that provide information on definitions, explanations, symptoms, and treatment of anxiety disorders. Don't visit every site; pick two or three good ones that give you the basics.

Purchase from a book store or borrow, from a library, two or three books on anxiety disorders. Don't take every book off the shelves. A little knowledge goes a long way and too much information is not a good thing.

The goal here is not to create worry about anxiety symptoms, but to understand them better. If you immerse yourself in too much reading material, you'll find that you are focusing too much on anxiety and that will only serve to increase it.

A little bit of information, just enough to lead to understanding, is sufficient to begin the process of gaining power and control over it. In this way, your anxiety won't control you, you will control it.

One way to gain information in a relaxed atmosphere is to watch a movie where the characters experience some of the same type of symptoms that you do. It allows you to see functioning adults living quite well despite their symptoms. These movies often depict characters that are able to make adjustments, overcome, or come to terms with their condition. A few examples are: As Good as it Gets, Analyze This, High Anxiety, and The Truman Show. You may want to view a movie before you begin reading anything, because it can set the tone for assimilating written information. The more relaxed you are, the easier it is to absorb and understand what you are reading.

Before you begin to read, find a calm and quiet space where you can read undisturbed and relaxed. It's better if you are alone in a peaceful setting. I like to read while I sit on my porch swing, especially if there is a slight breeze blowing. If the weather is uncooperative, then I sit by a window.

When you sit down to read the materials you've gathered, bring a highlighter and some Post-It notes. Better yet, get a Post-It highlighter that has the page tabs built in. As you are reading, highlight the areas that pertain to you. Use the Post-Its to mark pages you've highlighted so you can easily return to them. If you've borrowed a book from the library, just use the notes. The library might not appreciate the highlighted pages.

If you are like me, you'll soon find that you are highlighting every page. Your hand may get tired and you may run out of fluid and have to get another highlighter. This is where acceptance usually walks through the door with a blinding light. It's difficult to deny that anxiety may be an issue when the words are jumping out of the page saying, "This is me."

You may even find that you are unable to put the book down and read it all in one sitting, especially if it is well-written. Something magical happens when you recognize yourself in the pages. It's as if, finally, someone understands and has put into words what you could not. There's a sudden realization that you are not alone and it's okay.

According to the National Institute of Mental Health, approximately forty million American adults (eighteen percent) have an anxiety disorder in a given year. Most suffer from more than just one. That's a staggering statistic (say that three times, fast).

Take comfort in the fact that there is information and treatment available. There are others who understand exactly what you are experiencing that can offer support or assistance. This is important, especially since anxiety disorders are often misunderstood by those who have not experienced them.

In fact, many people with anxiety find that they are stigmatized. This can make anxiety even more difficult to deal with, especially if you blame yourself and have unrealistic expectations about controlling it. I have heard many of the following statements: maybe you need a vacation, you just need to learn to relax more, what in your life is causing you such stress, perhaps your plate is too full, you're doing too much, take it easy, try not to worry.

The reality is that it's not that simple. Everyday stress and worry can be controlled by simple means, but when you reach the disorder stage it's entirely different. In trying to educate those close to me so they can gain a better understanding, I use the following example:

imagine for a minute that every day, all day long, you can feel the blood coursing through your veins as it circulates. It creates a constant distraction to you that is difficult to ignore and you cannot control it. This is what it's like to have generalized anxiety. It's there, always, and it's unsettling.

Reading about others who truly understand can bring a great deal of comfort, and increase your own understanding of these ailments. After you have read all of your materials, highlighted pertinent information, and reached an understanding of what you are dealing with, then it is time to let go of denial and practice acceptance.

When you deny or fight anxiety it just gets worse. Leaning into it and practicing acceptance lessens anxiety. Understanding leads to acceptance and acceptance is the portal to moving forward.

Think of it in these terms: imagine that you cut your leg on a tree branch. You ignore it even when someone else points it out, putting it out of your mind. The sore begins to sting, and then throb, but you still give it no attention. It starts to ooze and becomes infected. When you can no longer ignore it, you seek treatment. If you do not, it will continue to get worse and the infection will spread. As you understand and accept that your leg can no longer be ignored and you take action to improve your condition, you begin to heal.

Acceptance allows you to approach the door to healing and to managing your anxiety. You will notice that when you reach the point

Chapter 4

Step 4

Reconsider

Step four asks you to reconsider your diet. This doesn't mean that you are expected to abide by a specific diet, or worry about what you eat. In reconsidering your diet, the main goal is to simply be aware of your eating patterns. Know what you eat, when you eat it, and how you eat it.

The function of food is to satiate hunger, fuel the body with energy, nourish the body, and keep it healthy and alive. Unfortunately, many of us eat unconsciously, and food is used to comfort, socialize, and serve as a form of entertainment. Try to remember this: whatever you put into your body has an effect, desired or undesired.

In order to reconsider your diet, it helps to think differently about food. This can seem difficult at first, but it becomes effortless and routine with practice. Roadblocks to success include family gatherings, social events, and stress.

Family gatherings, holidays, social or work-related events all revolve around food. Buffet style meals with tables full of food are the norm. You are encouraged to try a little bit of everything.

When the situation is uncomfortable or stressful, food and drink can provide comfort or distraction. So what do we do? We shovel another forkful in and pour another beverage down our throats. Hunger and thirst may be long gone, but eating and drinking keeps our hands and mouths busy, and releases emotional tension. For those of us with anxiety, it allows us to focus on the food rather than the feelings we may be experiencing.

So, the first and most important part of step four, reconsidering, is to become a conscious eater. Be aware of every morsel you eat and why. Pay attention to how you feel after meals or snacks. If you find this difficult, then keep another journal-a food diary. There's nothing like seeing it in black and white.

Try to eat only when you are hungry and do not eat to the point of fullness. Eat until the hunger has abated. Stuffing yourself like a turkey will only make you feel full, bloated, and tired.

It may be better to eat five or six small meals a day, rather than three hearty meals. Watch your portions. Don't heap a pile of food on your plate. Better yet, use a lunch-sized plate. Remember, it's not a bowl, it's a plate. The food is meant to be flat on the plate, not three-dimensional.

Change the way your meals are structured. If you like meat and potatoes, try using the meat and potatoes as a side dish and the vegetables as the entrée. Cover half your dish with vegetables. Split the other half into equal portions of meat and potatoes.

Natural, organic foods with the deepest coloring are best for you. These foods include most fruits and vegetables. Strawberries, blueberries, broccoli, and apples are all good examples. Foods with the least amount of coloring should either be avoided or eaten infrequently. Examples of these include bread, celery, and pasta.

Eating healthier foods in smaller portions will not only make you feel better physically, they'll give you an emotional boost as well. It'll also help to lessen symptoms of anxiety, especially if you have any feelings of guilt related to making poor food choices.

One of the most important changes you can make is to eliminate caffeine from your diet. Caffeine is a stimulant. It works as a drug in that it affects the central nervous system. It helps to keep you awake, but can also give you the jitters when taken in excess. Caffeine can increase anxiety, cause headaches, and create a general feeling of being unwell. If you have trouble believing what a difference this can make, try it for awhile. Eliminate caffeinated beverages for a couple of weeks and then try one again and see how you feel. Most likely, you'll feel jittery, anxious and restless.

If you truly enjoy coffee, soft drinks, or tea, and find them difficult to give up, then taper off slowly rather than giving them up all at once. Remember, you don't have to eliminate these drinks altogether, just the caffeine in them. It may take some time, but you will find that you get used to the change and develop intolerance for caffeine. Try herbal teas; chamomile is a good choice for relaxation.

I recommend drinking water all day long, four to six cups a day works well for me. Limit decaffeinated beverages to one or two per day. I have developed the habit of carrying a bottle or travel cup of water with me wherever I go. This prevents me from getting dehydrated or thirsty, and it ensures that I get plenty of fluids.

Stay away from processed foods and unhealthy snacks. Eat whole, natural, fresh foods whenever possible. Snacking on almonds and walnuts is better for you than chips and dip. Eating yogurt is a healthier alternative to ice cream.

When you crave sweets or salty foods, don't deny yourself, just make wiser choices. If you must have chocolate cake, then try something that tastes the same but is lower in calories, and smaller in size. One hundred calorie snacks can be found at just about every grocery store and there are many to choose from.

Sugar is also a big no-no when it comes to anxiety. Eating sugary foods or foods that convert to sugar in the body affect blood sugar and insulin levels. Soon after eating sugar you may feel a burst of energy, but it doesn't take long before it wears off and you crash. Eating sugar again can turn this into a vicious cycle. This cycle has a huge impact on anxiety. It's the crashing part of the cycle that causes the problem.

When you crash, you want and need food immediately. If you do not eat then the symptoms get worse. You get very hungry, anxious, irritable, shaky, have trouble focusing or concentrating, and have zero energy. Don't reach for the nearest sweet when you feel this way, although it can be tempting.

Complex carbohydrates and proteins last much longer in your system than simple carbohydrates or sweets. So, stick to these foods whenever possible. A slice of cheese or turkey is better for you than a cookie or potato chips. Carry an energy bar with you if there is a chance that you might skip a meal; it'll prevent you from grabbing a candy bar or convenience item at a check-out counter.

You may consider taking a class or reading a book on nutrition. Eating the proper foods will not only lessen your anxiety, it will improve your overall sense of well-being and you will be healthier.

In addition to diet, consider your environment. It helps to avoid exposure to pesticides and strong chemical cleaners. Try to purchase more environmentally healthy products. If you are painting or refinishing furniture, make sure you have a source of fresh air and take frequent breaks. Keep houseplants in your living area as they tend to absorb toxins and impurities in the air. I refer to this as my environmental diet because everything you breathe in or has direct contact with your skin can have an effect on the body. Whatever affects your body can affect your anxiety level.

This doesn't have to be a difficult or time consuming process. It also doesn't have to happen all at once. You can begin the process with baby steps and continue to move forward slowly. There is no hurry. Follow this step at a pace that is comfortable for you; a pace that lowers your anxiety level and doesn't add to it. Start with being conscious while you eat. The rest may follow naturally, with little effort.

Chapter 5

Step 5

Navigate

It is easy to get caught up in everyday activities, routines, and obligations without thinking about them. We run on automatic pilot, which leaves us feeling ragged, depleted, and stressed. The pace of our lives can be determined solely by us, if we choose to navigate.

The best way to take control of your life is by viewing yourself as navigator. Write a job description for this role, if necessary. What does this mean for you? If you allow yourself to become aware of how each and every day is shaped, then you can begin to take control of planning your own days.

Don't allow yourself to get caught up in a whirlwind of activities, especially if they continue for days, weeks, months, or years. Eventually, this will take a toll on you. If you ignore the signs and symptoms of exhaustion and stress and continue at an unhealthy pace, you may truly become unhealthy. Anxiety and panic symptoms can increase. Physical and emotional strain can lead to serious illness.

Making the decision to navigate your own course can be life changing. It's a simple concept, yet we often fail to do this. Our life is driven by "should" and we tend to ignore our own needs and wants. Ultimately, we find ourselves out of control. This is because we have given up control. We end up going through the motions, doing what is expected of us by others, and maybe even building up resentment along the way.

How many of us have heard or said, "I don't have time for that."? Well, of course you don't, not if you don't make the time for whatever "that" is. How can you find time when your schedule is so full?

Begin to navigate, prioritize, and create your own time-table. Once you realize that you can manufacture the time to navigate a simpler life, you are halfway there.

This may all sound good in theory, and taking that first step can feel a bit intimidating, especially if you don't know where to start. That is what step five is all about, so let's begin.

To navigate a simpler life, begin by de-cluttering. Get rid of items that you haven't used, or have no use for. Start with one area of your home. It can be a shed, a garage, a closet, a kitchen, a drawer, anywhere. Whatever space you begin with, empty it completely. Look over each item and decide if it is something you can part with. Use three empty boxes for placing your unwanted items. Label the boxes:

one for charity or hand-me-downs, one for yard sale or flea market, and one for trash.

My number one rule for this exercise is this: if I cannot identify what the item is, I don't absolutely need it, or haven't used it in a year or more, out it goes. I can actually remember a time when I was boxing up all my household goods to move, after being in a home for three years, when I found two large boxes that I had never opened. I had no idea what was inside. Obviously I never missed the stuff, so I took it all to charity (I did peek in the boxes first-there wasn't anything there for me to keep).

Once you've cleared an area, organize what you have kept and put it away. Create some empty space so your storage area is easy to access and items are easy to locate. Once that is done, move to the next area. Continue, over a period of time, until you've been through your entire house. It might be helpful to begin in one corner of the house and work your way to the opposite corner; that's what I did.

Next, establish a rule that whenever you bring in something new, something old must go. You may be surprised how freeing this is. If you don't do this, then you may need to go through the entire de-cluttering process every few years in order to stay organized and free from the accumulation of unnecessary "stuff".

Owning a lot of material goods can really bog you down. Even worse, it can cause stress and symptoms of anxiety. Your "stuff" can take over your life. Anyone that has tried to find a flashlight in the dark can attest to that.

Pay attention to how you feel when you start this process. It may seem like a daunting task, one that you'd rather avoid than face. This is a sure sign that it is time to begin. If you open a closet or drawer and can't find what you want, or things tumble out of their own accord, then it is time to de-clutter and organize.

It may increase your stress and anxiety when you begin the process, but these feelings are temporary. Once you are done, you will feel an enormous sense of relief.

You will also save time and aggravation, because once you are finished, you will have touched everything you own and found a place for it. When you know exactly where everything is, there's no more endless hunting for a screwdriver or pair of scissors.

Next, make a to-do list. Write down anything that needs your attention. Does a room need painting? Do you need to shampoo or replace a carpet? Does the back door or railing need to be repaired?

Make an agreement with yourself or someone you live with that you will tackle these items one at a time. Pick a time frame; one per week or per month. Don't set yourself up for failure. Keep your expectations realistic. If you set up unrealistic expectations or fret over the list you will only add stress and anxiety to your life.

Start with a small list, accomplish those tasks one-by-one and then make a new list. If the list is too long, you won't know where to begin. Try prioritizing your list; number items one through five, or one through ten.

In order to accomplish these tasks and find time for yourself, take a look at what an ordinary day looks like for you. Creating more space means eliminating unnecessary obligations, or restructuring your calendar.

First, combine trips whenever possible. Don't go to the cleaners, run home, and then go out later for groceries. Plan your activities to save time by scheduling in advance. Navigate your day. Eliminate unnecessary trips.

Second, take a look at what a typical day consists of for you. Is there any task you can erase from your day? Do you absolutely have to pick up your dry cleaning today, or can it wait for tomorrow when you go to the bank and market?

There was a time in my life when I was not working outside the home and my children were in school. My days were mine, but I gave them away. I volunteered, belonged to three quilt groups, did all the housework, paid all the bills, did all the gardening and yard work, drove the children to all of their activities and appointments, joined a book club, and attended girls' night out events. If you asked me to do something, the answer was always yes. I was a people pleaser. Besides, I had the time because I wasn't working, right?

Clearly the answer is no. I could limit volunteer hours, join one club instead of three, ask family members for help around the house, and learn to say no. I did, but then I got a part-time job, then another, went back to school, and then got a full-time job. My life was a mess and my anxiety was at an all time high. Eventually I learned to balance my life and I am much happier and less stressed because of it.

Try not to fall into the trap of doing too much, like I did. Don't overload your schedule. Decide what is important to you and prioritize and limit your activities. If you want to take a new class or join a new group, drop something else that is less important to you at this moment. You can always pick it up again, later, if you choose. Create a balanced schedule, but allow time for spontaneity too. You don't have to attend every meeting, every month. It's okay to take a break because you desire a night at home, or a walk in the moonlight. You only live once, so you might as well enjoy as much time as you can while you are here.

Eliminating activities, items, and obligations from your life can be like removing a giant boulder from your shoulder. You may just find that you have time to relax and do something you actually enjoy. If nothing else, navigating a simpler lifestyle will reduce stress and anxiety. Don't take my word for it. Try it.

Chapter 6

Step 6

Exercise

When you are young, exercise is nothing but fun. The chance to run, ride bikes, play sports and outdoor games, go for long walks, and even mowing the grass, are welcomed warmly. As you get older, your perspective changes along with your metabolism. At least, for me, it did.

Although exercise is not a four letter word, once I hit forty, I'd cringe when I heard it. Just the thought of adding exercise to my already busy day filled me with dread. At that point I wanted to simplify my life, not add something to it. Ugh!

I was always much more comfortable when exercise was incorporated into my day, rather than purposely exercising just for exercise sake. It always felt better when my exercise was productive, like gardening or putting up a fence. The idea of walking a treadmill or using an elliptical machine only added to my anxiety and made me feel unwell. I had no tolerance for vigorous exercise, and no desire to join a gym.

What I have come to learn is that there is a very good reason for this trepidation. Exercising just for exercise sake is difficult when you have anxiety because your mind wanders too much; it gives you too much thinking time. While on a treadmill, my anxiety would build. I'd get hot, dizzy, nervous, shaky, and feel awful. This is because I was stuck inside my own head, thinking about the past, the future, and focusing way too much on how nervous I felt about how I felt physically.

When you are gardening, putting up a fence, hiking, or are engaged in any form of exercising that requires your concentration, then there is no thinking time. You are entirely focused on the task at hand. You are in the "zone". This level of focus brings about a calm, pleasant feeling that leaves anxiety behind.

There are many types of exercise that can bring us to the zone and help to alleviate anxiety. Certain forms of exercise can even teach us to remember that feeling of being in the zone so we can use it in moments of anxiety when we are not exercising.

I have several types of exercise that I will recommend in this chapter. You can choose one of these, or create one of your own. I have practiced all of them and find that calm, soulful, meditative forms of exercise are the most beneficial in dealing with symptoms of anxiety.

The first one on my list is yoga. Yoga is well known for its calming effect, and I have found it to be a wonderful tool in dealing with anxiety. There are so many benefits to practicing the art of yoga.

Yoga is calming, meditative, balancing, grounding, smooth, and fluid. It can also be restorative. There are several different types of yoga and many different methods of practicing. You can join a class, work with a personal trainer, get a book, purchase a DVD, follow a yoga television program, or subscribe to a yoga magazine. Before you choose a method or type of yoga, do some research on the subject. The internet is a great place to start; you may even find a recommended class in your community.

Tai Chi is another form of movement that has a calming or meditative effect. It is enjoyable to practice and leaves you feeling very free and relaxed. You can research this form of exercise on the internet as well. You may even find that you have a Tai Chi center in your area.

Both yoga and Tai Chi will tone, shape, and balance your body. They will also help with your posture and the way that you carry yourself. Ideal side effects include: less stress, less anxiety, increased self-esteem, self assurance, and inspiration.

Another form of exercise that works wonders is walking, especially if you practice meditative walking. If you haven't walked in some time, start off with short walks and increase distance and time as you build stamina and confidence. It's important to be comfortable with your walking distance.

Find a safe, pleasant route. Somewhere close to home is better as you'll be more inclined to continue if the site is convenient. Try the streets of a small city or town, a path in a park, around a small lake, or a country lane. Remember to dress comfortably and wear good walking shoes.

Try not to get lost in thought when you walk. If thoughts come into your mind, then let them flow, but be aware of them. Look at your surroundings; study the leaves, the stores, the homes, the flowers, whatever you find along the way. Feel the movement of your body as you walk, pay attention to how it moves. Listen to the sounds, the birds, cars, and the wind. Walk at a good pace, not too fast or too slow. This is a walking meditation. Practice this three times a week.

Dancing in the privacy of your own home is another great exercise. Put on some comfortable clothes; I prefer pajamas and bare feet. Turn some of your favorite music on. Close your eyes. Listen to the music; identify the instruments, the lyrics, and the sound. Find the beat and let your body flow to the rhythm. You may be surprised what this can do for you. I call this method of dance, dancing meditation. It's a great tool in helping me to let go and be free of worry or anxious thoughts. Music is soothing to the soul. Listening to music and moving to the sounds is a very peaceful and relaxing experience.

When I am doing something physical that is producing results and also serves as a form of exercise, my spirits and energy level rise. When I practice calming and meditative forms of exercise, I feel at peace and relaxed. My anxiety flows away like low tide and I develop a memory of these feelings. This memory allows me to garner feelings of peace when I am stressed. The benefit transcends itself to other life experiences.

If you feel that the form of exercise that you chose heightens your anxiety, or if you feel overwhelmed by the obligation of exercising, then try one of these forms. You may find, for the first time, you are more relaxed during exercise. You may even enjoy it more. Don't underestimate the effect this can have.

Exercise doesn't have to be a dreaded chore; it doesn't have to be difficult to find rewards. Choose a form that works well for you, one that reduces stress and anxiety. Variety is good too, experiment with them all, on a rotating basis. Remember to check with your physician before you begin any new exercise program.

When exercise helps you to feel better physically, and emotionally, it can have a profound effect. It may not just change your view of exercise; it may give you a new perspective on life in general.

Chapter 7

Step 7

Yield

To yield means to bring in or give way to. In step seven you are asked to yield to your creative side. Everyone has one, and everyone is capable of tapping into it. For some it's right there on the surface, easy to find and utilize, but for others it is hidden and might take a little more effort to bring out.

Many of you may already participate in a creative activity, but not of your own choice. An example of this is a young boy who is taught to play the trumpet. Maybe he picked it up in school, encouraged by parents and /or teachers to try an instrument. He may or may not be very good at it. He may not enjoy the trumpet, but can play it well. His true creative side may be hidden below the surface. Perhaps he never had the opportunity to know what it is, or maybe he took an interest in something when he was young and was discouraged from pursuing it. Maybe it was his idea to learn the trumpet, but he's just bored with it and would like to try something else. Perhaps he's not bored with the trumpet, but the thought to try something else has never occurred to him on a conscious level. Somewhere in the back of his mind there may be an unconscious or ignored desire to play the piano, to paint, or to write.

If you find yourself thinking that this doesn't sound right or apply to you, and that you have no creative side; fear not, you are wrong. It is true that everyone has a creative side. Everyone has done something creative in their life, even if it is not recognized as such.

I can remember a time when I was sixteen years old and I put a minor scratch on my father's car. I was ready to panic, thinking that I'd get my car privileges taken away, or worse, have to pay to get it painted. When I showed it to my little brother and asked him what I should do, he came up with a creative plan. He painted over it with his model car paint. Maybe this wasn't the best solution, but it was pretty creative. Ahem, don't try this stunt at home; it may be hazardous to your health.

The good news is that you can develop your own, individual creative side. There are many different ways to accomplish this. I will offer tips and techniques to do so in this chapter.

One of the first things you can do is to make an appointment with a life coach. A life coach can help you to uncover your creative side and discover what form it will take. They can guide you to develop specific skills, or offer advice on how to pursue your creativity. This can be especially helpful if you are stuck in a rut or routine, or if your creative talents are hidden. An appointment with a life coach is not expensive; it's not something exclusively for the wealthy. It's actually quite affordable. In many cases, one visit is all it takes to get you started.

Visit your local library or book store and look for books on creativity. Find ones that contains an aptitude test. A career test may even help, because it can point out your strengths and weaknesses, and spark an interest that you didn't know was there.

Sometimes our creativity is blocked because we are stuck on auto-pilot and routine has consumed our life. Making simple changes to break away from this can be enough to get your creative energy flowing. It can be something as easy as turning off the television for an hour a day and using that time to engage in a new activity.

Another method is to create a list. Try writing down a number of new things you'd consider trying. Write down as many ideas as you can and see what appeals to you the most.

Take a day trip to a museum. Look at each exhibit carefully and see if anything sparks an interest for you. You never know what may move you to create. Maybe you'll see an antique violin and develop a curiosity that motivates you to take lessons. I had a museum experience once that surprised me. While looking at the exhibits, I glanced down at the floor and noticed the floor tiles. They fascinated me and stimulated an idea for making a quilt. Sometimes, our motivation can come from the most unlikely places. Trust your instincts and listen to that inner muse.

Look in the newspaper for local groups in your community. There are groups for so many different hobbies and activities. To name a few: knitting, quilt making, bridge, model trains, chess, tatting, writing, and painting. Many of these groups allow visitors to attend a free meeting to try it out. Attend one and see if it's a good fit for you.

Try challenging yourself to participate in something new and different, something you may not have considered before. Volunteering is a great way to do this. Find out what non-profit agencies are in your community and what they do. You might find that you like telling stories to children, building houses for the homeless, developing a newsletter for an agency that doesn't have funds for staff to do so, teach crafts to the elderly, the list is endless.

Take a class at the local community college or through your adult education department. Acquire a course listing to see what classes are being offered. Get a copy of the syllabus for the class that interests you in order to see exactly what will be taught for the duration of the class. Sometimes the class description can be vague, and you will be disappointed if it doesn't meet your expectations. The syllabus can prevent that from happening.

Encourage the right side of your brain, your creative side, by using it. Doodle on paper, put together a jig-saw puzzle, play a board or computer game, do a word or number puzzle. Grab a bag of assorted items and see what you can make of it. An example would be a pinecone, some paint, a string, and some glitter could make a nice ornament. It could also end up as a tiny heap in your trash bag if this type of creative outlet is not for you, and that's fine. You may not find your creative niche on the first try.

Practice relaxation. The best ideas can come to you when you are still. I can remember a time when I was sitting outside on my porch swing, quietly enjoying the nice weather, when I noticed a long stick on the ground. I picked it up, turned it over in my hands and decided that it would make a great walking stick for hiking. I bought a few carving tools, took off the bark, and smoothed the stick. It was simple, but serviceable, and I enjoyed the process. Now, whenever I hike, I'm on the lookout for large sticks.

Watch children playing, this doesn't mean stalking a playground. It just means that when you happen to see a group of children playing, notice what they are doing. Children are naturally creative and watching them may spark an idea. Searching through pictures of your own children or looking through their toys can stimulate creativity. When my children grew out of cribs, their little Mother Goose mobile served no purpose, but I didn't want to throw it away. I took the little figures off of it and made them into Christmas ornaments for the family tree. It wasn't anything fancy, just some string and a few flat, painted, wooden pieces.

Go back to your journals, from the first step, and see if you find any inspiration there. Maybe you've scribbled a few drawings or have written a poem. Listen to music while you do this, maybe a song will inspire you to something.

The great thing about yielding to creativity is that it can serve as a form of therapy. While in the process of creating, your mind is focused, you are concentrating on the task at hand. Your troubles and worries are left behind and negative thoughts and anxiety are washed away.

Being creative gives you the opportunity to step outside of obligations and responsibilities, and take part in something new and exciting. It takes you away from everyday stress and allows you to participate in the world in different ways.

Yielding to creativity provides so many benefits. It helps to minimize symptoms of anxiety and stress, it helps to develop self confidence, improves overall health and well-being, and it is fun. Most of all, being creative takes us to a place where we can discover who we really are.

Chapter 8

Step 8

Practice

Step eight is about discovering the practice of present moment awareness, or living in the moment. This is a concept that comes easily and automatically to some, but takes quite a bit of practice for others. Sometimes, it comes in a moment of enlightenment or epiphany. It may be the single, most important step you take on this journey.

In simple terms, all it means is to practice the art of being. Be in the moment and experience all it has to offer. Pay attention to all that you are doing, hearing, saying, seeing, and feeling, always.

Most of us live our lives unconsciously. We move from moment to moment without paying attention. We get stuck in our own heads, lost in thought about the past or future. For sufferers of anxiety, it is common to be trapped in thought, especially negative thought patterns. In fact, you can be so trapped in thought that you don't even know that you are thinking.

For example: how many of us have ever truly taken a shower? We're under the stream of hot, comforting water, but our minds are wandering through our day, week, or through the years. There have been many times when I was so lost in thought during a shower that I could not remember if I had washed my hair or not. A million thoughts would run through my head, seemingly all at once.

The problem with being stuck in the thought process is that it is the super highway to stress, anxiety, and panic. Over thinking and over analyzing are huge contributors to anxious thoughts. What's worse is how we react to these thoughts. Negative or repetitive thoughts can lead to panic if we let it. The "should" and "what if" begin to dominate and we ignore the truth of the present moment. We try to shape how past moments could have been different or how we might behave in future moments. This robs of us of the moment we are in now.

Think about your walk into work from the parking lot, or from the street or driveway into your home. Are you thinking about your day, evening, your work, or the next day? Is your mind busy? Are you conscious of your footsteps as you walk? Do you notice your surroundings?

The next time you take this familiar walk, let go of all of your thoughts. Look at the path you are taking. Notice what you see, hear, feel, and smell along the way. You might find that this path is not so familiar after all. Maybe you'll see that the sidewalk is cracked, the shrubs have grown, the mulch is fresh and new, there are beautiful flowers and busy bees, the snow is shoveled in a pattern, or ants are making a new home along the side. The list can be endless. The benefits of doing this will follow you through the entire day.

To better illustrate this concept, imagine what would happen when lost in thought, you fail to notice a shift in the concrete on the sidewalk. You trip on it while walking into work, carrying your morning coffee (decaffeinated, of course). The coffee goes flying, you wrench your ankle while falling forward, your glasses break as you fall, and the temple rod cuts a gash in your face. Half your work day is lost because you need a couple of stitches, and you must get your glasses repaired. This is not an extreme example (may automobile accidents are), it actually happened to me. Had I been paying attention to where I was instead of where I was going, I may not have fallen at all.

Here's another example: imagine that you are at work, experiencing a typical day. Your supervisor approaches you with an ambiguous comment. The comment is not explained and body language does not identify its meaning. You begin to think about the comment and try to understand. You wonder if the boss is upset, if you've done something wrong. Instead of asking for clarification or letting it go, you over analyze; you ask a co-worker what it might mean. You think about it a lot, so much, in fact, that by the time you make it to work the next day and notice that your boss is in not in the best of moods, you think it has something to do with you and the comment that was made. You wonder if you might get fired, so you are careful to be on your best behavior. You come in early and leave late.

When it comes time for your performance evaluation, your supervisor states that you've been doing a terrific job and tells you to expect a raise. The boss tells you that your early arrival and late departure are appreciated, but not necessary. You get a day off for your efforts.

You begin to realize that all the worry and concern was for nothing. It was your own negative thoughts that took over and changed your experience. All that time spent analyzing and worrying was wasted time. You notice that you relax a bit more, your posture and attitude changes. It was all a big misunderstanding that could have been avoided. How did it happen? Were you simply lost in your own thoughts during this conversation?

During a conversation, it helps to listen intently, notice body language and facial expressions, and ask for clarification on anything that leaves you with a question or concern. Clear, open, communication during the moment at hand can eliminate this type of anxiety and over analyzing.

Changing this pattern doesn't mean that you need to beat yourself up every time you get lost in thought. There is no need to drive thoughts away. Fighting the thoughts will only serve to increase anxiety and stress.

It's not the thoughts themselves that really create the problem; it's that you do so unconsciously. Simply being aware of these thoughts can have a dramatic effect. When you know that you are over thinking and your thoughts are spinning out of control, you can begin to acknowledge the process and recognize it for what it is. It's just mind chatter.

The best way to deal with this is in the moment. Watch the thoughts come and go, allow them to be. When the thoughts dissipate, bring your awareness back to the moment at hand.

One good way to practice living in the moment is through meditation. There are many forms of meditation. You can read about them in a book, magazine, on the internet, or you can make up your own. Meditation allows you to clear the mind, rest the body, and find a place of peace within yourself.

When you learn to live in the present moment, life can take on new meaning. Creative outlets will open. You will get to know others better and enjoy them more. Tolerance, non-judgment, empathy and acceptance become easier as you accept each moment. A new joy will emerge and anxiety will slip into the background.

Chapter 9

Step 9

Encouragement

There is so much misunderstanding about anxiety and panic, that it can be difficult to find supportive encouragement. Even encouragement itself is often misunderstood.

"Hey, pal, get over it," is not a form of encouragement, even when the speaker thinks it is. It can be discouraging to hear the same sort of misguided encouragement time after time, especially if it comes from someone close to you. Ironically, this type of support only adds to stress and anxiety.

Anyone giving this type of encouragement usually sees anxiety and panic as coming from external sources, and their advice will include eliminating sources of stress from your life. This is not the least bit helpful.

True encouragement comes from those who know and understand that anxiety, from an anxiety disorder, comes from within. Educating family and close friends to this fact can help to eliminate the added stress and anxiety that comes from this misguided form of support.

Anxiety and panic are not disorders that you can talk yourself out of in one step, or by taking one pill (ahem--that's why this book has twelve steps). It may take a series of efforts to make your anxiety manageable.

Seeking and finding encouragement is an important step towards managing anxiety, and it may take some time and patience to find the right type of encouragement and support for you.

Individual counseling is an option that I strongly recommend. It's a great place to start. Sharing your experiences with a neutral party, that is paid to listen to you, serves to reduce anxiety and stress in and of itself.

Get a recommendation for a good therapist from other professionals in the community (nurses, doctors, lawyers), someone who works with them frequently. Choose someone that knows you well enough to suggest a good match. A good counselor will actively listen to you, and help to push you forward at a comfortable pace.

Therapists can also help to provide insight into behaviors, triggers, or reactions that you may not recognize. Be open to suggestions, as this may be the best form of encouragement you'll receive.

A therapist may be able to help you find a support group in your community. Support groups are a good illustration or indication of just how many others share the same experiences. A good support group will welcome everyone warmly, leave no one standing alone, and encourage participation of all members.

Groups that incorporate activities are ideal, especially if the activities include methods for dealing with anxiety. If the group tends to focus on symptoms, experiences, and negative thought patterns, then it may not be helpful. It's good to share these commonalities, but not to dwell on them. Remember, you are looking for encouragement, so groups should offer the practice of behavior techniques or activities that reduce stress and anxiety, not ones that add to it.

After all, how helpful would it be if a group approached a first time visitor, with social anxiety, and asked them to get up in front of everyone to relate their story? Hello? Is anyone home? Is this type of encouragement helpful or therapeutic in any way? Knowing how to support and encourage members appropriately is a vital part of any group.

Group activities might include a diverse number of items, on a rotating basis. Some examples are: role playing, meditation, positive thinking, cognitive behavior techniques, the twelve steps of Journey to Peace, yoga, Tai Chi, dancing, guest speakers, crafts, games, pet therapy, deep breathing, humor, anything creative and uplifting.

The type of encouragement I look for when dealing with anxiety, is one that fills my spirit with courage and hope. Courage to move forwards despite anxious feelings, and hope that anxiety eventually becomes manageable with time, effort, and support.

Assistance does not have to come from a formal support group for people with anxiety. Support and encouragement can be found in many different types of groups, even in the most unlikely places. Experiment by trying different groups, until you find the right fit.

If a group has an empathetic, caring, team spirit, and the members bond, then support and encouragement can be realized just by participating. Group activities can lesson stress and anxiety, and help you to capture that feeling to carry through the day.

As you grow and change, so do your needs and desires. Changing groups as you grow is acceptable and appropriate if that is what you need to continue forward. Joining a group does not mean that you must stay for life.

To better illustrate this concept, I'll give an example. Let's say that you take a creative writing class that you enjoy so much, you join a writing group when the class is completed. Eventually, you leave the writing group and join a book club.

The book club turns out to be a good fit for you because you share a lot in common with the members. You form lasting friendships and find a support system that provides the encouragement you need. Friends from the group support your writing, help you through difficult, anxious times, encourage you to participate in book discussions, and lift you up to a new potential. You find, during meetings and outings with these friends, that anxiety slips behind you.

In today's world of technology and the internet, help can be a keystroke away. You can join an online support group and chat with members every day, if necessary. This method can be a great ice-breaker for someone with social anxiety--socialize through the computer before you do so in person. It's a wonderful way to pull someone out of their shell. You may even be able to find a sponsor on the internet.

Sponsors can be helpful and can be found through almost any formal support group. They serve as a daily check-in person, and a friend you can call on in an emergency. You'll want someone that understands and empathizes, but does not enable. Read about sponsor relationships on the internet to learn more about the role they play.

When you find someone you'd like to ask, ask them gently and respectfully. Communicate relationship expectations from the beginning. Remember to celebrate victories with them as well as sharing trying times.

Churches are another option for finding support and encouragement. Most ministers are trained in counseling and provide religious based assistance. Churches also have many different community groups. There may be a Bible study, or volunteer group that meets your needs.

Don't forget to encourage yourself. This may be the greatest gift you ever receive.

Chapter 10

Step 10

Attitude

Developing a positive attitude can help you to create the life you want. The first step to achieving a positive attitude is to accept the idea that you are in control of your thoughts, and that you, alone, can create your own happiness.

Know that a positive outlook is healing and helps to rejuvenate the body and mind. Remind yourself of this frequently.

When stress and anxiety take hold, or negative thoughts crop up, think positive thoughts, even when it may be difficult to do. Expect that you won't always be able to maintain a positive point of view. There will be bumps in the road along the way; however, you will be able to open your new toolbox of positive attitude enhancers and get back on track.

The best tool in your box is the perspective shaper. Take it out and use it whenever you encounter negative or worrisome thoughts. When these thoughts begin to take shape and you start to feel symptoms of stress or anxiety, be aware of exactly what you are feeling and what the cause or trigger is. Typically, these negative thoughts come from holding onto one perspective, or one way of thinking about an experience. Shape that perspective by considering viewing the situation from another angle.

Here's an example: Imagine that you are upset because you didn't hear from your best friend on your birthday. There's no note, no card, no call, no contact. Usually, this is a person you can depend on to remember and recognize your special day. For the past few years, you've celebrated together by going out to dinner, lunch, or an outing. The more you think about it, the more you feel hurt and disappointed. You begin to feel sad, angry, and put off. Maybe you start to think that you may be thinking selfishly and perhaps there is something wrong with your friend. It could be that your friend is sick, or in the hospital. You worry about this all day long, going back and forth with your thoughts.

In a moment of clarity, you take out your perspective shaper and realize that all this worry and thinking is meaningless and unnecessary. You begin to think, silly me, one telephone call can resolve this. So, you call your friend and find out that you had forgotten about your friend's out of town visitors.

When you are able to see the situation from another perspective, the stress and worry disappear. You are free from the symptoms of anxiety and are able to let go of the consistent, negative thought patterns.

Another tool that works well is distraction. Find something else to do that occupies your mind and keeps you busy. Preferably, make this a positive activity so you can build on your positive attitude. Visit the library and choose a new book to read, go for a walk in the park, work in your garden, or watch an up-lifting movie.

Your grateful journal is another useful tool. Take it out and read through it; remind yourself of the things you are most grateful for. Start a new list. It can be something as simple as being grateful for the feel of the soft carpet under your feet. You may be surprised how this activity contributes to a positive outlook.

Appreciating the little things is another tool that works wonders. Take time to look up at the clouds, like you did as a child and see if they form a particular shape. Look at the leaves on the trees and notice the different shapes and vein patterns. Watch the flowers sway gently in the breeze. Allow all thoughts to fall into the background as you simply enjoy the moment.

During stressful times or difficult events, think back to some of the best times of your life. Remember what it felt like. Capture that feeling and transfer it to your current situation. This will help you to switch perspectives and allow you to make better decisions, based on clearer thinking.

Surround yourself with positive people. Vow to stay away from relationships that bog you down, or enable you to remain in a negative or anxious state. I realize that this can be difficult, especially if this person is your spouse, sibling, good friend, or parent. If it's a relationship you feel that you must maintain, or choose to, set up some proper boundaries to protect yourself.

It takes two to continue the dance routine of a relationship. If one person changes their behavior, then the other will eventually make adjustments to accommodate. It may take some time, and the other person may resist, but ultimately, when your perspective is changed and you become aware of the dance, it will no longer have the hold on you that it once did.

Bring laughter into your life. Watch a funny movie, visit a comedy club, or read the comics in the newspaper. Find an amusing book, or attend a comedic play. Learn to see the humor in everyday activities, and try to add a little humor to each day.

Volunteer your services to a local non-profit agency. Giving to others is a positive experience that you can carry with you for a long time. The opportunities are limitless, as many non-profit agencies are always looking for volunteers. A few examples are: helping to build homes for the homeless, teaching an adult to read, helping someone to learn the English language, taking shelter animals for walks, and tutoring children.

Prayer can be very helpful. You don't need to go to church or believe in God to practice prayer. Simply look to a higher power, whether it is a god, or a deeper, more spiritual part of you. It doesn't really matter. Realizing that there is something or someone beyond the suffering part of your personal experience serves to bring you to a more accepting place. The art of letting go contributes to a positive outlook and helps to lift your spirits. Give yourself a break. Human beings were not meant to be perfect, and perfection isn't all it's cracked up to be anyway. Leave perfection to God, or the higher part of you that resides deep within.

Developing a consistent positive attitude can take time and practice, but it is well worth the effort. You can create a new version of you by adopting a positive attitude. Your outlook, health and well being will be improved, and you will have even more to be grateful for.

Chapter 11

Step 11

Create

This could be the easiest step in the book. It may also be a lot of fun. The goal is to create a relaxing, therapeutic area that you can go to in times of stress. A personal, calming, soothing space is an invaluable resource. Ideally, you will have more than one.

The space can be indoor, outdoor, or both. It does not have to be a large area. Your spot can be a room, a garden, a portion of a room, a converted closet, a stairway, or a shelf in a room. Take your time choosing a locale. It's important that the space you choose is a place that brings you comfort and is easily accessible.

The area you choose is to serve as your personal, private oasis. It'll be your soft place to fall, a place where you can ground yourself, regroup, rejuvenate, find solace, relax, and experience peace.

If you live in an apartment, room, or a small area, and feel you don't have the room for this, think creatively. Perhaps you can use a shelf, a bureau top, or a chair by a window.

One important element to consider is color. You'll want your space to contain a soothing, warm, soft color. Medium or light tones work best. Examples are: pale blue, mauve, sand, melon, teal, and soft green. Choose a color you like, as long as it is not too stark, bright, dark, or neutral. You can use paint, wallpaper, artwork, or cloth to add colors. If your space is a chair by a window, add a throw or quilt to the chair. If you are using a shelf, place a piece of artwork above it, on the wall, or paint the shelf. For adding color to an outdoor space, consider planting flowers or putting up a birdfeeder or birdhouse.

Make sure your oasis is well organized and free from clutter. It is best when neat, but lived in. The space need not be empty, stark, or barren, just not cluttered.

Find a comfortable seat for your space. It can be a sofa, soft chair, a corner of your bed, floor pillow, swing, bench, rocker, glider, or whatever you prefer. I have a brown leather sofa in front of my fireplace that I love to sink into. The minute I'm sitting back in the seat, I begin to relax. This is the type of seat you want, one that brings instant comfort.

Add some of your favorite things to your space. If you collect seashells, put some in a pretty vase, or bowl and set in a visual spot. If you are an avid reader, keep a basket of books by your chair. If your space is outside, make a small garden with pretty stones and a small fountain.

Lighting is important. You'll want the soft light that comes from a small lamp, candles, or a fireplace. When deciding on a lamp, choose one with character, something different that interests you, or try making one of your own. Try a solar light for your outdoor spot.

Scent is also important. For your outdoor spot, add aromatic flora. Indoors, use an air freshener, scented candle, or fragrant houseplant.

Soft music is a pleasant addition. When outdoors, listen to the natural sounds of the landscape, and hang a set of chimes. Indoors, keep some of your favorite music handy. If you play a musical instrument, keep it by your chair.

The idea is to create an atmosphere of peace and relaxation. Tap into your creativity to make this space uniquely yours.

I have a couple of spaces that work well for me. My favorite spot is the swing on my front porch. It doesn't matter what the weather is, because I find peace whenever I sit there. I go out to it often, sit, and gently swing back and forth as my feet rock on the floor. I look out at the trees, grass, flowers, birds, squirrels, bunnies, and deer. While listening to the natural sounds I feel enveloped in peace and warmth. It is easy to relax and enjoy the moment. When I am ready to rise, I sometimes do a walking meditation around the outside of the house before I head in.

While I don't recommend using a car as a personal refuge, I'd like to site it here as a good example of creating a personal, individualized space. Have you ever noticed a car that stands out in the crowd because the owner has plastered it with personality? Personal belongings dangle from the rearview mirror. Stuffed animals abound on the front and back dash. Bumper stickers cover the entire rear of the vehicle, or one makes a political statement. Personalized license plates and add-on features all work to reveal a piece of character or personality. Seldom do you see a seventy year old grandmother driving a Hummer with twenty-four inch wheels. Why? Mostly because the average person chooses an automobile that they are comfortable driving, something that suites their personality and lifestyle.

View your space in much the same way, as an extension of self. This area is for you. Allow for creativity in making it yours. Go shopping at a flea or farmer's market for unique hand-crafted items, or make some of your own. For example, try to avoid purchasing a non-descript candle holder from a department store; this is your opportunity to create.

There were times in my life when the kitchen sink or ironing board served as this space for me. They are quiet, contemplative, soothing tasks. Ironing with soft music playing in the background, or while watching a calm movie is relaxing. The ironing board and basket of clothes takes up room that creates a little cocoon around me. No one in the family will invade that space, not unless they want to do the ironing, and there isn't another soul in my household that enjoys ironing, so I'm safe.

If your kitchen sink has a window above it, then curtains can add color and you can place a candle on the windowsill for adding scent and color. Again, most family members won't disturb you while doing dishes; they just may get recruited to help. Volunteer to do the dishes every night and you just may find that this becomes your favorite personal space.

Your space does not have to be anything official, fancy, or expensive. It is meant to be a place of respite. It can be a quiet meditative area, or a spot for unleashing creativity. You can have one or several areas. The only thing that is truly important is that the locale is uniquely yours and you spend time in it every day, even if it is only five to ten minutes. Take the time to create your own space, and reap the rewards by spending time there to relax and enjoy the peace and serenity.

Chapter 12

Step 12

Extravagance

Now it's time for the real fun, step twelve. Here you are encouraged to be extravagant. Treat yourself to a special luxury, something that you would not ordinarily participate in.

If your lifestyle is hectic or frantic and your to-do list is long, then it is especially important that you create some time to lavish yourself with indulgence.

The good news is that when you pamper yourself everyone around you benefits. Engaging in an activity that lifts your spirits and makes you feel good shifts your general attitude. Anxiety and stress take a step backwards and your ability to face whatever may come your way is enhanced. Problems become challenges. Concerns and issues no longer seem insurmountable.

My own perspective changed about this many years ago when I was, gulp, selling cosmetics at home parties. I had a large party scheduled in the inner city, in a poor neighborhood where money was scarce and people made do.

When I arrived there were twelve women waiting for a free make-over. Excited chatter filled the small dining area. While the ladies took their seats, the men swept the children away to another location. During the evening there was a lot of talking, laughing, sharing, and questions. Everyone was having a good time and they said so often.

I was happy to provide the free make-over and didn't expect to sell much product. In fact, I felt a little guilty because the cosmetics were not inexpensive. One of the women must have sensed my discomfort, maybe it was my lame attempt to sell. Anyway, after I packaged up a number of sales for the evening, she approached me to purchase a lipstick color she had tried and liked. She said that I should relax and sell as much as I could. She told me that these ladies don't ever get the opportunity to treat themselves like this. The men in their life had arranged this get together. They were given money to spend and wanted to use it to purchase a few extravagant items because it made them feel good.

She explained that this time was theirs to participate in a shared activity with loved ones, and to create memories. This was the men's way for thanking them for all they do for their families. The products they purchased would prolong the feelings and memories of that night.

Every time they used their new cosmetics they would feel pretty, sexy, and flirty.

A couple of months went by and one of the women from that party called to reorder a lipstick. She told me these ladies still carried their smiles and stories of that evening to family events. The men in their lives felt good for providing the night for them, and the women weren't as grumpy or frustrated when the children misbehaved.

So, the lesson here is when you treat yourself to something extravagant, all those around you reap the benefits as well. You certainly can't put a price tag on that. Maybe that lipstick wasn't so expensive, after all.

One of the things I like to do to treat myself is to get a massage. It feels extravagant to me so I don't do it very often, well, not often enough. Maybe I should do it more often, it can be thought of as a necessary part of health care, can't it? You might want to check it out; go ahead, try a massage.

Body work has more benefits than I can list here, but I'll attempt to share a few. The best benefits I get from massage: it has taught me how to relax, let go, and capture the feeling of relaxation to take with me and use when needed most. It took me a while to get there; it didn't happen with my first or second session.

The hardest thing for me to do was to let go of my head. I wanted to hold it up myself and had trouble letting someone else hold it up for me. Until I experienced massage I never realized how much work it is to hold my head up and maintain control over my physical body.

To let go of control of the physical body and allow someone else to work it into a state of relaxation is the paradise of extravagance. I highly recommend it to anyone.

Another generous option is to get a pedicure or manicure, or both. This is an especially good treat if you have an important social event to attend, like a wedding. It's relaxing to have your hands and legs massaged, and to have someone else trim and shine your nails. Plus, when you get middle-aged like me, you can't reach or see your own feet any more. It's better to pay someone else to do it so you won't cut a toe off or something.

Purchasing a new outfit and/or a pair of shoes that do not come from a dollar store can be fun and exciting. Treat yourself to a trip to a nice mall, elegant shop, of fancy department store and pick up an item or two, or ten.

Take a vacation; go somewhere you've always dreamed of going. It can be a mountain, a tropical island, or an amusement park. Even a day trip can be nice. Visit an aquarium, zoo, or see a play or movie. Take a hike to a beautiful waterfall, or attend a fair. The options are endless.

If your budget is small and it requires you to save for an extravagance like this, there are still many things you can do to treat yourself in the meantime. Examples might be: go out for an ice-cream sundae, get a new hair style, take a bubble bath by candlelight, take the time to read a book you've always wanted to read, play a round of golf, or whatever appeals to you. Choose an activity completely out of routine.

You won't regret this effort. In fact, you are bound to repeat it several different times in various ways. You may even feel like a whole new you has emerged, and that is worth any extravagance. Enjoy!

Afterward

Congratulations on completing the twelve steps. By now you have gathered enough tools to assist you in dealing with anxiety, panic, stress, and life in general. I trust you will keep this book as a resource and refer to it often.

My goal in writing this book and developing the twelve steps is to reach out and help others who share some of the same experiences that I have. I sincerely hope I have achieved this end result.

Cognitive Behavior Techniques

On the following pages you will find twelve cognitive behavior techniques that will be helpful to utilize during times of stress. It may also be advantageous to start or end your day with one of these practices.

~

Inner Light

Find a quiet, comfortable spot to sit, away from distraction.

Set a candle in front of you.

Light the candle and gaze at the flame as you sink into your seat and begin to relax.

Imagine that this fire is the source of peace, a place to find your inner light.

Allow all of your troubles, worries, and thoughts to melt away with the wax.

Continue this practice for five to ten minutes or until you feel calm and relaxed.

~

~

Soulful Music

Practice this technique when you are alone in your home.

Turn on a piece of your favorite music.

Stand up and close your eyes.

Feel the beat of the music deep into your soul.

Imagine the music carrying all of your troubles away.

Open your eyes; raise your voice and sing aloud.

Push away all thoughts and worries.

Sing loud and clear.

Allow yourself to let go and enjoy two songs.

~

~

Delightful Dance

Follow this technique alone, or with a loved one, close to you.

Turn on some soft, uplifting music.

Close your eyes and feel the rhythm.

Begin to sway, move, and dance to the beat.

Listen for specific instruments.

Pay attention to the lyrics.

Allow yourself to get lost in the moment.

Enjoy the motion and movement of your body.

Let all thoughts slip away.

~

~

Nature Trail

Take an imaginary walk down a trail in the woods.

The trail has soft sand under your feet.

There are no hills or inclines.

Trees provide shade and dappled sunlight along the way.

As you move forward you leave all of your anxiety and stress behind.

The birds are singing.

Native plants carry blossoming flowers.

At the end of the trail a comfortable bench and cool breeze await you.

~

~

Waterfall

Imagine you are in a tropical paradise.

The air is warm and a slight breeze persists

You stroll through the woods on a well worn path.

A light waterfall can be heard in the distance.

The sound gets more prominent as you get closer.

You walk up a gentle incline that curves and declines again.

As you turn the curve the waterfall comes into view.

The pool beneath it looks inviting.

You approach and step into the cool, refreshing water.

The water is waist high; your feet touch the soft sandy bottom.

There is a flat, worn shelf below the falls.

You swim over to it and sit, relaxed.

You allow the cool water to cascade over your head,

down your body and into the pool below.

The fresh, clean water washes away all of your negative thoughts and

stress,

as they are carried down the stream at the end of the pool.

~

~

Mindful Breathing

Sit or lie down in a comfortable position,

one where you are sure to stay awake.

Focus your attention on your breathing.

Breathe normally.

Do not take a deep breath or attempt to control your breathing.

Feel the breath move through your body as you inhale and exhale.

Empty your mind of thoughts.

Pay attention to each breath.

If thoughts come, simply be aware of them.

Let the thoughts come and go.

Gently bring your focus back to your breathing.

Continue for five to ten minutes.

~

~

Pet Therapy

Spend some time with your dog or cat.

Sit calmly and quietly and allow your animal to come to you.

Begin to give the animal attention by gently stroking behind the ears.

Move to the side of the face, then the top of the head.

Work your way down your pet's body, providing a gentle massage.

Use a relaxing, soft hand as you work towards the tail.

Focus all your attention on your hands.

Notice how it feels to provide a loving touch.

Pay attention to your pet's reaction.

After the massage, spend some playful time together, and go for a

~

Letting Go

Lie down in bed, on your back.

Bend your knees or place a pillow under your legs for back support.

Rest your head on a pillow.

Concentrate on your toes as you tighten them for a couple of seconds

and let go.

Move to your feet, tighten and release.

Work your way up your body.

Tighten and release each section of your body,

one at a time.

Your calves, knees, thighs, pelvis, back and stomach,

chest, shoulders, arms, hands, neck, face, and scalp.

Focus on how you feel as you tense and release.

Let your body sink into the mattress and completely relax.

Rise slowly and carry that relaxed feeling with you.

~

~

Shower Recharge

Get a soft, fluffy towel and hang by the shower.

Take off all of your clothes.

Turn the water on to a comfortable, warm spray and steady flow.

Step into the spray and feel the rejuvenating power of the water.

Allow the stream to wash over you as you revel in the warmth.

Massage your scalp with your fingertips as you shampoo your hair.

Feel the soft, smooth, silky texture of your clean hair.

Use a softly scented body wash to cleanse your body.

Take your time massaging the soap into lather.

Enjoy how the lather caresses your skin.

Feel the healing properties of the water as you rinse off.

Turn off the faucet and wrap the fluffy towel around you.

Pat yourself dry, slowly.

Smooth body lotion on your legs and arms.

Use a gentle moisturizer on your face.

Take pleasure from your clean, relaxed, rejuvenated body.

~

~

Body Scan

Sit up straight with your feet firmly planted on the floor.

Put on some soft, relaxing music.

Scan your body head to toe.

Pay particular attention to your posture.

Are you shoulders back and relaxed?

Are you holding you neck and shoulders tight and close to your head?

Are your hands tightly fisted?

Are you grinding or clenching your teeth?

As you scan each area of your body, relax and let go.

Practice this often.

~

~

Time Out

Spend some time at home in solitude.

Turn off the television, radio, telephone, and all bright lights.

Light a candle or turn on a softly lit lamp.

Sit quietly in a comfortable chair and practice meditation.

Clear your mind of thoughts and concerns.

Repeat to yourself that you are calm, relaxed and at peace.

Feel your body relax.

Sink deeper into your chair.

Feel your breath and heartbeat slow as you repeat your mantra.

Allow yourself this time-out from everything.

~

~

Floating Petal

Visualize yourself sitting at the edge of a gently flowing stream.

Picture the water trickling over smooth stones,

worn from the constant motion of the water.

Imagine the sound of the stream as quiet and soothing.

You are beginning to relax and enjoy the moment.

Place a leaf or flower petal in the stream.

Watch the petal as it floats away.

Believe that the petal is carrying all of your stress and anxiety with it,

leaving you in a state of total relaxation.

You are calm and at peace.

Capture this feeling and take it with you as you go.

~

About the Author

The author has a BS in Professional Communication from Old Dominion University, with an emphasis in strategic communication. She is an anxiety sufferer with more than twenty years experience in dealing with members of the health profession, conducting personal research on the subject, and practicing various techniques.

Peg has previously published magazine and newspaper articles; this is her first book.

Printed in the United States
144768LV00005B/1/P